Mountain Feuds
of Eastern Kentucky

Copyright © 2023 by Commonwealth Book Company, Inc.

All rights reserved. No part of this book may be reproduced in any form or by any means without the prior written consent of the publisher, excepting brief quotes used in reviews. Printed in the United States of America.

ISBN: 978-1-948986-67-0

Mountain Feuds of Eastern Kentucky
THE REYNOLDS & THE WRIGHTS

NOAH M. REYNOLDS

Commownealth Book Company
St. Martin, Ohio

INTRODUCTION

I will now attempt to give the reader a brief sketch of my fore parents. My grandfather, Noah Reynolds, was born in Russell county, Virginia, where he married Chaney Stone, who was a very small woman, weighing from seventy-five to eighty pounds.

To their happy union were born ten children, five boys and five girls. My father, Henry Reynolds, being the oldest child, induced his father to move to Kentucky, where he bought a small tract of land near the mouth of Boone Fork, of the north fork of Kentucky River. This being a very sparsely settled section of the mountains, game was plentiful. The coves and small bottoms were fertile, bringing abundant crops of corn and garden vegetables. The neighbors being kind and generous-hearted, would lend a helping hand to anything they could see their neighbor needed, without the asking, everybody going to church on Sunday and worshipping God according to the dictates of their own conscience.

My father, Henry Reynolds, at the age of twenty-one years, married my mother, Matilda Baker, age fifteen years, the daughter of Henry Baker, a noted Methodist preacher, to whom were born nine children, three boys and six girls, of which I (Noah Reynolds) was the oldest. He being a brick mason by trade, handed down the same art and skill to his three sons, the same art and skill he had acquired from his father (making and laying brick). Working at his profession, brick laying, and tilling the soil, he raised his family to the years of maturity in peace and harmony with all mankind.

I, Noah M. Reynolds, the oldest son of Henry Reynolds, was born Feb. 13th, 1866.

My brother, John H. Reynolds, whose life was interwoven so closely with my own, as the reader will see later on, was born Aug. 29th, 1882.

I, or we, as all the other small children of our neighborhood, went to school barefooted, played ball and such other games as was for the amusement of school children, and were surpassed in skill by none.

Our home was where the mining town Seco now is. Going three miles to school where Neon now is, me being the oldest, had to look after the home affairs, failed to get the education my brother John received, he making a school teacher in later years.

I want the reader to know and understand we were raised and instructed by as good parents as ever lived in the State of Kentucky, or elsewhere.

We were taught to do unto all men as we would they do unto us. I, Noah Reynolds, being the oldest boy of the family, as I have stated before, at an early age learned the brick mason trade, working with my Uncle Ange Reynolds. We built the first courthouse that was built at Clintwood, Dickenson county, Virginia, I being only thirteen years old. At the age of seventeen, we made the brick and built the courthouse at Hazard, Perry county, Kentucky. I also helped to build the courthouse and jail at Whitesburg, Letcher county, Kentucky, where my brother, William H. Reynolds, is now jailer. I continued to lay brick, building chimneys in divers places in Eastern Kentucky and Southwest Virginia, farming, trading some in stock, which leads up to the time of which I am about to relate.

Mountain Feuds of Kentucky

FRANCH AND EVERSOLE WAR

In Which About Seventy-Four Men Lost Their Lives

Commencing in about the year 1882, this feud existed principally in Perry county, Ky. One of the worst battles fought during the series of battles between the factions of this feud was at Hazard, the county seat of Perry county, Kentucky, one faction occupying the courthouse which I have mentioned helping to build, the other was in dwelling houses, stores and anything convenient for men to get behind for protection from bullets. In this battle twelve men lost their lives and several were wounded. There was fighting almost every day in which some one was either wounded or killed. In this war, Clabe Jones, a great mountain feudist, played an important part. There was also a terrible feud existing in Rowan county, Ky. Morehead, the county seat, was the center of this feud, in which there was from eighty-five to one hundred men killed. The next feud of note was in Breathett county, Ky., Jackson being the county seat, and commonly known as the "Bloody Breathett Feud." In this terrible feud one side of the participating factions originally came from Russell county, Va., the same county my grandfather came from. There has never been any accurate account kept of the actual number of men killed during this great struggle.

THE HATFIELD AND McCOY FEUD

The next feud of importance was waged along the Kentucky, West Virginia and Virginia state lines, known as the "Hatfield and McCoy Feud." This dreadful feud was fought by heartless and fearless men on both sides. In not only this but all the other feuds which I have mentioned I could give the names of many of the men which we commonly call bad men. But for the respect I have for both the living and the dead I will leave that part off.

OLD CLABE JONES AND JOHN WRIGHT FEUD

The next feud of importance, which was fought mostly under my personal observation, was fought under the leaderships of "Devil" John Wright, who commanded one faction, and old Clabe Jones, commanding the other. This feud started from the murder of Linvil Higgins, who was killed at a point where Hindman, the county seat of Knott county, Ky., now is. This man Higgins was killed by three men, one of which was Wm. S. Wright, who later on was the man who started the trouble between himself and me, causing his own death.

For this Higgins killing, there were several indictments made.

Wright and others refused to submit to the law. Dolph Drawn, a deputy sheriff in and for Knott county, Ky., organized a band of men of about thirty in number, marched into Letcher county, Ky., to apprehend these parties accused of the killing of Higgins

("Daniels Hill Fight"). On their way they were fired on from ambush at a point known as Daniels Hill by the Wrights' band and a general fight ensued, in which several men were wounded, one of which (the noted Talt Hall) received a severe and painful wound in the shoulder. He belonged to the Wright faction; and a man by the name of Short, who was with the Drawn side, was shot with a shot gun. John Wright commanding his side of the fight used a shot gun. In this fight not only were men shot, but several horses were also shot, one of which, a very fine horse belonging to Dolph Drawn, was killed on the spot. Which later on John Wright paid for—regretting the killing of a fine horse. The Drawn party, being stampeded, retreated in bad order, going back to Knott county, each man by himself. On their return home they joined Clabe Jones, he refusing to accompany Drawn on his raid into Letcher county, because Drawn insisted on making the raid on horseback in cavalry form. Clabe being an old mountain feudist understood the nature of his opponents, telling Drawn he had better crawl on his hands and knees into Letcher county, he knowing the cunningness of John Wright, Talt Hall, WM. S. WRIGHT, and others of his gang. After banding under the leadership of Clabe Jones another raid was planned, Jones advising and instructing his men as how he would conduct his warfare, going after Wrights in the name of the law, while Wright, as shrewd a craftsman as ever commanded a bunch of men in our mountains, had his men organized in the same manner.

Clabe Jones and John Wright each had rewards for the other, signed by the governor of Kentucky. Clabe Jones, mustering his men together, set out to capture or kill John Wright and his men. Laden with guns and ammunition, traveling during the night and hiding in the mountains during the day. But on arriving at Wright's stronghold ("Fort Wright" as it was called), learned that Wright had gone to Knott county, looking for him. Jones and his men now, on failing to find Wright, returned home in the same manner as they had come—watching for Wright during the day and traveling by night.

SECOND RAID BY JONES ON "FORT WRIGHT"

Jones, on arriving home in Knott county, learned that Wright was also at home on the head of Elkhorne Creek, in Letcher county. Wright having failed to find Jones on his raid had returned home also. Jones takes his men and traveling by night and laying up by day, as he had done on the first raid, arrived at "Fort Wright" in the night. Arranging themselves as best they could, concealing themselves behind trees, rocks and such other obstructions that they could find, waited for daylight to come.

On the first sight of a man (Bill Bates) stepping out of the "Fort," Jones and his men opened fire on him. Talt Hall and several men who were in the "Fort" held Jones off until John Wright, who was stopping with a lady friend some three hundred yards away, came to their rescue. The shooting

Mountain Feuds of Kentucky

lasted for two hours and was almost a continual roar. Jones, seeing his helpless condition to either kill or capture any of Wright's gang, retreated! Strange to say, but true, no one was killed, but some were slightly wounded. Wright, pursuing Jones, came up with him on Mill Creek, a tributary of Rockhouse fork of Kentucky River. Here a desperate battle was fought, in which John Wright lost a man. Wright had this man carried away and buried, as it was the way each side of every faction of the feudists to bury their dead and let nobody know it if possible.

Each side seeing the great danger and impossibility of capturing the other, decided to rest.

One of Jones' braves (Bill Cook) surprised and captured Wash Craft near the mouth of Millstone Creek. Summoning J. Wash Adams as a guard, he put Craft on a horse behind Adams and started on their way to Hindman jail. Arriving at a point on Rockhouse just below the mouth of Beaverdam Creek, Craft snatched a 38 revolver from Adams and fired five shots in succession, killing Cook instantly, liberating himself and making his way back to and joining his friends.

John Wright, hearing of the capture of Craft, mustered eighteen men and went in pursuit of Cook. Going a near way to cut him off they came across parties carrying Cook's dead body.

Learning Craft had killed Cook he went back with his men to "Fort Wright." This feud lasted on and on for several years, one and two men meeting at a time and fighting with guns and pistols, generally to a finish.

Mountain Feuds of Kentucky

Continuing on and on, other troubles grew out of this feud until one hundred and fifty men or more were killed. I have only mentioned a very few of the names of the parties who took part in this great struggle. It may be strange to the reader to learn that all parties tried in court for this trouble came clear.

ANOTHER BAD TROUBLE

This happened at mouth of Boone, one-fourth of a mile up Kentucky River from where the Daniels Hill fight occurred, which I have already mentioned as being between Blain Combs on one side and W. S. Wright on the other. They met in the night-time. A desperate battle ensued, in which Combs lost two men. Then Combs chased Wright one mile up Boone's Fork to where Wright lived, the place where Seco mining town now is.

The next trouble of particular note was waged between W. S. WRIGHT on one side, and Lige and Sam Wright on the other. This trouble grew out of W. S. Wright accusing Lige and Sam Wright of killing his dog. W. S. Wright mustered a band of fifteen men and went in the night to the home of Sam and Lige Wright, broke down their door. The fighting, shooting and killing commenced. Andy Wright and BILL WRIGHT, known as "Old Bill" Wright being killed and "Black Bill" Wright was severely wounded. The W. S. Wright band ran from the scene of battle, leaving their dead and wounded laying where they fell. Sam and Lige Wright were indicted in court at Whitesburg, Ky. Sam Wright broke jail. John Davis Bentley, deputy sheriff, caught Sam Wright, and on his way to jail with him, W. S. Wright, hearing of Sam Wright's capture, waylaid them and shot the prisoner through the back, severely wounding him.

Later on Sam and Lige came clear in court. Then W. S. Wright swore that "Black Bill" Wright, who was a brother of Sam and Lige, had betrayed him and got his men killed, and sent him to the penitentiary for five years. He died in prison.

Now, coming to the time in the history of the lives of myself and John Reynolds. I at this time, was about nineteen years old. At this age I married one Miss Maggie Sergent, she being the same age as myself, the daughter of Stephen Sergent, who lived on Rockhouse Creek, and to our happy union there has been born eleven children, of which we have raised ten to man and womanhood. After I got married everything moved along smooth and nice.

My father had given me a farm and a branch called Big Branch, which emptied into Boone. My uncle, Cuge Reynolds, owned a farm at the mouth of this branch. Some time later uncle Cuge sold his farm to one W. S. Wright. This man, W. S. Wright, was a very determined, overbearing and vicious man—a man who had almost done as he pleased with his neighbors, and ruled the courts, on account of the fear the people had for him. He could prove whatsoever he wished to carry his case in court, and if he happened to fail he would resort to arms. So the people generally were afraid of him. The sound of his name was a terror to the whole country. After he had moved to the uncle Cuge farm I was determined to get along with him and I let him have his way. For a long time he would do everything he could think of that he thought would interrupt me. His idea was to get my land for nothing.

THE FIRST TROUBLE OF NOTE

W. S. Wright and Jas. Johnson, his son-in-law, were cutting timber just below my house. W. S. Wright called me to come down where he was; said he wanted to see me on business. I went down and asked him what it was. He said, "I understand you claim a poplar tree that stands near the land line between you and me." "Yes," said I, "my father does. It is not mine, as I have not got my deed from father yet. You and father will have to settle about the tree, I guess." "So far I don't think there is much man in you, anyway," he said. He knew how to raise a man's temper. Then said I, "I am a smaller man than you in size but more man than you."

He then said, "You are a liar, and I can whip you in a minute." Coming towards me with a large knife in his hand, I backed off from him. He followed me to the fence. I jumped the fence and went on up the road to my home, with hot blood, but no way to help it but let time cool it down. We all knew he was a bad man and consulted together how to get on with him. We decided to let him have his way, which was a great mistake.

THE NEXT TROUBLE

I had cut some rail timber near the line between him and me. While I was away from home he split it into rails and laid them in his fence. I missed my timber and saw the rails in his fence. When I met with him I asked him why he had taken my timber. He said he had not taken any of my timber. Then, said I, "I'll see to that. I will just law you. I didn't think you would steal. I thought you had hired someone and that they had gotten them through a mistake." He said, "Go on home; I'll be up some of these days and settle with you about it."

"No," said I, "if we settle it, it will be to-day." "Well, I'll be up this evening and we will settle." I went on home, believing I would have trouble with him. Sure enough, in the evening he came up and called me. I had heard before this that he had said he was going to whip me over the timber. I had a small gun which I dropped into my side coat pocket, and went on to where he was. On getting near him I asked him if he was satisfied he got my timber. "Yes, I hired one of the Potters. He thought it was my timber. I will pay you for the timber. How much is it worth?" I told him and he paid me and said, "You are all the time giving me trouble. I guess I had as well give you a good whipping and then you little sorry thing you will let me alone." Slipping up his sleeves, he came toward me. I backed a step and drew my pistol and pointed it at his face. He threw up his hands and said, "Don't shoot me; I'll not hurt you." About this time

George Vance stepped from a clump of bushes near by with a revolver in his hand. I jumped behind a large poplar stump and said, "You two rascals leave this place or I will kill you both." They immediately left, and I heard Wright tell Vance that "That little devil would have killed me if you had not been there."

SEEKING THE ADVANTAGE OF ME

Some days later I was passing by his home—the road passed right by his yard gate—he said to me, "I acknowledge I did you wrong." I said, "That's all right; the good book says we must forgive." If this acknowledgment had been real, or from his heart, things might not have happened as the reader will see later on. In the fall of 1897, I made a brick-kiln on the lower part of the farm—a part of the farm my grand-father had given to his son, Steve Reynolds. We being friendly at this time, I built him (W. S. Wright) a chimney and did some other small jobs for him. That year I was doing some work in the lower end of the county, and while I was away from home, he, W. S. Wright, hauled my brick kiln home. When I came home I went to his home and asked about my brick. He pretended to fly mad, stepped into his house, got his big Winchester and invited me up the road, which invitation I accepted without pleasure. I then took a warrant for my brick and he waived the case to court. The case came up and I, thinking he had no plea, made no special preparations for trial, not knowing much about lawing at that time, being inexperienced. Not thinking he would swear anything to beat the case, I only had witnesses to prove he hauled the brick away.

He went on the stand, swore he had bought the brick from me when we were all alone, and beat me out of my whole brick-kiln.

In this same year W. S. Wright, his wife, Lettie Wright, and their boys, began killing my hogs, geese, etc., wherever they could find them, killing six good hogs and putting them in a big hollow poplar log.

A few days later my brother John and I were repairing some fence when my little boy came and said, "Wright is killing your big sow." Not feeling good over the loss of my other property, which they had killed, brother John and I took our guns and went down where Joseph and Johnny Wright, W. S. Wright's sons, were dogging my hog—had five dogs on her. I stood nearby with my gun while my brother John killed three dogs; one dog running near the Wright boys, I told my brother not to kill it, being afraid he might shoot one of the boys. About this time Wright hung some gates across our road, which had been a passway for a good many years. I appealed to the court to prohibit him from fastening us up, as we had no other way to get out from home, except down the hollow by Wright's house. The court gave me a right-of-way through his land, but allowed him to still keep the gates across our road.

A SHOOTING AFFRAY

In April, 1898, it was now our time to plow our corn ground. On returning home from the mill, W. S. Wright's boys and Jim Bates, his nephew, were plowing in a field adjoining a field which I intended to cultivate in corn. I was standing in my door—Jim Bates called me "Old Clabe Jones" (who was a noted feudist of Kentucky), and said, "What are you going to do this evening, Clabe?" I said "I am going to plow, but I don't know what it is to you." "You will see what it is to me," he said, "You will not plow this evening; I'll see to that."

I had bought me a 44 revolver. I saw trouble was coming. I went up to my mother's home and got my brother John to come and help me plow. We went to the field to plow and there was a fence which divided my field from that of W. S. Wright's. I had my big pistol buckled on me and John Reynolds had a small pistol in his pocket. We plowed several rounds and nothing was said. They would make it convenient to meet us at the fence. We all stopped to rest. Jim Bates said to me, "Clabe, what are you doing with that big pistol? You won't use it. I guess I had better just come over and take it and knock your d—— brains out with it." I said, "Me and my pistol is tending to our own business, and you had better tend to yours." By this time he had got on top of the fence. Then said I, "Don't you get inside of my field. If you do, I will shoot your heart out," taking my pistol from my holster. He had two rocks in his hands. He jumped off the fence, and as he straightened I fired at him, wounding him in the left shoulder. The blood spurted when he fell. I turned to shoot Tilden Wright and he threw up his hands and said, "Don't shoot me; we haven't got any guns." By this time Bates had recovered and, taking a new notion, jumped the fence back out of my field. Then I looked out in the field, saw W. S. Wright and his wife, Lettie, coming. He asked if anyone was killed. I told him "I think not; I have only broke one's wing." I said, "Mr. Wright, it looks like you could control yourself and family better than what you are doing." He then, seeking the advantage of me, told me that I shouldn't be bothered any more. They did not law me for this, but I could catch them trying to get opportunities to take my life.

TROUBLE OVER SCHOOL ELECTIONS

Our neighbors and friends insisted on my brother, Wm. Reynolds, to make the race for school trustee. He consented, and W. S. Wright declared himself a candidate against him. The election went off and my brother Bill got every vote cast but three. Wright had three sons-in-laws. I just made the remark that his sons-in-laws had beat him. His boy hearing me say this, Wright became enraged at this and his defeat, and said he intended his boys to give me a good whipping.

One day I was passing W. S. Wright's, and on going through the gate, just in front of his dwelling, Tilden Wright, the oldest son of W. S. Wright, was hid behind the gate post. I had a 44 Winchester rifle, model 73, on my shoulder. As I opened the gate Jim Bates attracted my attention, and the first thing I knew Tilden Wright had grabbed hold of my gun. Then at it we went. He was much larger than I, and it took every bit of nerve I could muster to hold on to my gun. A part of the time he had me down and part of the time I was on top. It was just who would and who could. This was a terrible struggle with me. I thought he was out-winding me. Almost exhausted in the struggle, I made a desperate effort to wrench the gun from him and almost succeeded. Getting enough control of the gun I got the muzzle turned toward him—the gun fired, the bullet grazing the side of his head. Then, somehow, we both fell, Bates grabbing the gun. He didn't know how to work the gun and I ran away, saving my life, and thinking I had probably killed Tilden. On my way up the branch home I met my mother. Seeing me muddy and bloody, she asked what was the matter. I told her and she went on down where we had fought. Finding my gun laying on the ground, she picked it up and brought it back. It was unharmed.

TROUBLE ABOUT OUR SCHOOL TEACHER AND JOHN REYNOLDS AND WM. WRIGHT'S FIGHT.

Our school trustee hired my cousin, Morgan T. Reynolds, to teach our school. W. S. Wright being mad at the whole generation of Reynoldses, swore Morgan T. should not teach the school. Writing Morgan a letter, he said "If you teach this school you will teach it over my dead body." Morgan, knowing the kind of man he was having to deal with, and knowing his reputation for having killed several people, his disposition as to having his way in everything he undertook, bought himself a Winchester, carried it with him to his school and kept it in a rack made for the purpose in the school house. My brother John, now a boy about seventeen years old, determined to get an education, started going to school to cousin Morgan. He had to pass W. S. Wright's house on his way to and from school, as the reader understands was the only way we could get out and into our home. On John's return home from school one evening, Wm. Wright, Jr., a second son of W. S. Wright, was on the road. He said to John, "Hold up, I am going to whip you, you damned — —," calling him an ugly name. Wright was a large man and Reynolds a very small fellow. Wright, having rocks in his hands, Reynolds said, "William, if you all don't let us alone some of you will get killed." Wright, not thinking of Reynolds having a pistol, made a dash for him. John drew his revolver and fired, glancing his head. Wright, falling to the ground, said, "Don't shoot anymore, I've quit." W. S. Wright was enraged by this trouble and went to a justice of the peace and procured a warrant for brother John, charging him with shooting and wounding, with intent to maim, disfigure and kill. John, on hearing of the warrant being out for him, went and gave himself up to the justice. The day was set for trial, witnesses summoned, and everything in readiness for the trial. Wrights failed to appear, and Reynolds waived his trial to court, awaiting the decision of the grand jury.

W. S. Wright mustered fifteen men and went to the Millstone Gap, expecting us Reynoldses to come back that way. I was sick in bed with the mumps, unable to go to John's trial. So Wrights, giving us out, came back that way, meeting John and mother in the road. On seeing Wright's band of armed men, John left the road and took shelter behind a large oak tree. Wright's men dismounted from their horses. John raised his gun to his shoulder, intending to sell his life as high as he could. Sam Wright, one of W. S. Wright's old and tried friends, was in the front ranks. Seeing John's position, he called to him saying, "Don't shoot; we only want to talk to you." John replied, "I have no talk for you. If you don't mean to hurt me go on and let me alone." So they went on. To make it more plain for the reader to understand Wright's intention, will tell you they didn't want to kill the boy by himself—they wanted to catch myself, my brothers, William and John, and our cousin, Morgan T. Reynolds, in a place where they could waylay and kill us all together. As I have stated, I was in bed sick when I heard that Wrights had gone with fifteen men to waylay my brother. I got out of bed, buckled on my pistols, laid my big Winchester on my shoulder and started in pursuit, not feeling able to stand on my feet. On my way up the mountain, I had to lay down several times to keep from fainting. Meeting my brothers William and John, we consulted together, they telling me the direction in which Wrights had gone. We decided to cut them off before they reached their place of safety. But they had passed before we could reach the point where we expected to encounter them.

Court came up. The grand jury investigating John's case, finding no charge against him he was released.

Some days after court I was on my way home from my mother's when in a short distance of my home a shot rang out and a bullet, just missing my head, struck a rail in the fence. Then a second shot was fired, passing so close to my head that it knocked me down. Looking in the direction from which the sound of the shots came could see no smoke. They were shooting with smokeless powder. Then I ran as fast as I could towards the house which, I guess, was a pretty rapid pace. There were six shots fired at me. As I went through my yard gate a bullet passed near me and struck in the ground near my little boy, throwing dirt in his face and knocking him down. I never found out for sure who did this shooting. Soon after this, I received news that one W. T. Holbrook had joined Wright's gang.

One night soon after I had received this news, W. T. Holbrook called at my gate about bed time. He hallowed "Hello." I told my wife to go to the door and see who it was. She asked him who he was. He said "A friend; is Noah at home?" She said "Yes." He said, "Tell him to come out. I want to see him." She asked him again who he was and he replied, "A friend." I was standing near a window and raising my revolver called to him to come in. "I know who you are." He said, "Don't go to shooting, I am your friend." I met him at the door with my pistol in my hand and took his 12-gauge shot gun from him and laid it in a rack.

I told him to take a chair and tell his business.

He began to talk, his voice quivering as though he knew I was on to his racket. He said, "Noah, old fellow, I am in trouble. This evening, while I was sitting on my porch, some one fired a shot at me, the ball just missing my head, burying itself in the wall; and I believe it was W. S. Wright. I knew you didn't like him—thought you was my friend and would help me to find out something about it. I want you to go with me and eavesdrop his house. If we can not, we will go on over to Bill Johnson's (a near neighbor to Wright); you know he is a man that often makes threats before he does anything."

I said, "I can not go. Times are very critical with me. I will not go out at night. I don't wish to take up any more trouble—I have enough trouble of my own. You can stay with me tonight and look after your business in the morning." He said, "No, I must go back home tonight. They will be uneasy about me." "I hardly think so; you will stay with me tonight. It's bed time and you can lay in that bed and I will lay in this." I knew he was there to kill me. I watched him close and neither of us slept any. Morning came and I was anxious to get shut of my visitor. While my wife prepared breakfast he tried to talk in a very friendly way.

After breakfast he asked me for his gun. I gave his gun to him and I followed him into the yard and said to him, "Now you are all right, I don't want you to bother me any more." "What do you mean by that," he said; "I am your friend." I said: "I know more about your business than you think I do." He turned pale, and walked off down the road some distance and darted into the woods.

In the evening he and W. S. Wright were seen going down the creek together.

Soon after this I went to the store at the mouth of Millstone and returned home a different way, as providence so decreed. I soon learned that W. S. Wright, W. T. Holbrook and James Johnson had planned to waylay me, thinking I would return the way I had gone. I procured warrants for their arrest, and after considerable trouble, got them caught, they refusing to surrender to the officers. After consulting with "Devil" John Wright they went with him to town and surrendered. On having their trial they were bound over in a bond of $500 each, on the confession of Holbrook.

One morning in the early winter of 1899, I went to my barn to feed. I found my mule had been stolen. As there was a snow on the ground I could see signs as to which way it had been taken. Thinking it had been done by W. S. Wright, or some of his clan, to decoy me into their hands, I went up to my brothers', William and John, to get them to go with me in search of my mule. We went down the road until we came in sight of W. S. Wright's house. We saw my mule hitched in his yard. We consulted together as to the best means or way to get the mule and we decided to go on and let brother Bill get the mule, as they weren't so mad at him, he never having had any particular trouble with them. He had no gun when we got to the yard gate. As there was no one in sight I started to go in and get my mule. Then Lettie Wright, wife of W. S. Wright, appeared and said, "Don't you come in my yard; I don't allow dogs in my yard." I said "I am going to have my mule." She said, "I will turn it out to you, but don't you come in my yard." She then brought the mule to the gate, pulled her bridle off and turned the mule loose. I caught the mule and was putting my bridle on it when Tilden Wright stepped from behind a shop house with a shot gun pointed at me. Brother John at the same time leveled his gun on him. Brother William took the mule, and about this time Jim Bates came from behind the dwelling house with a shotgun in his hand. We then started, or rather backed, over a bank into the road. They followed with their guns presented, we having our guns cocked and leveled on them. All parties were afraid to shoot for fear it would cause the other to be killed. We backed on up the road with our guns presented, and as I was nearing a bank in the road, which would give me some advantage of the ground, I backed over a cow that was laying in the road. As the cow was getting up her head came between Wright and me. He discharged his gun at this instant, shooting the cow in the head, putting about forty buckshot in her head and turning her heels in the air. I fell to the ground and using the cow as breastworks, fired three shots in quick succession. And as he went through the crack of the fence he filled his face full of splinters. At the same time John was shooting at Jim Bates.

Wright and Bates finally ran behind a bank

for safety. We went on up the road to our home.

Soon after this W. S. Wright organized a band of men and came near my home about 9:00 o'clock at night and commenced firing into my house. John and I got in one part of the house which was built of logs, and fired from windows at the blaze of their guns. The shooting lasted about twenty minutes and then ceased. We then kept a watch all night. Morning came and we cautiously went on the hill where they had been shooting from. We found their signs and lots of blood showing somebody had been hit. In an evening or so my wife and I had started to the barn to feed and milk, when about half way there a shot rang out from the hill, just missing us and hitting a log nearby. My wife dropped her bucket and said, "Let's get to the house." I fired two shots in the direction the bullet came from. I went on and helped milk, feed, etc. I never knew who fired the shot.

ANOTHER PLOT TO STORM MY CASTLE

I was informed by a special friend that W. S. Wright had called his men together again to make a raid on my house. On the night of the 28th of January, 1900, not wanting to fight in my house, left home at dusk and went over to Nat Bentley's and stayed all night. I came back to my mother's on the 29th. Wright, with his men, had been at my home, fired several shots into my house, found I was not at home. I learned later on that Wright wanted to kill my wife and children and burn my house. This has already been sworn to and is on record at Frankfort, Ky.

Mother asked John and I to leave the country. She was afraid we would get killed. I told her we didn't have much money and we would be in hard luck away from home. She then insisted that we go to Morgan T. Reynolds and borrow the money and she would pay it back. We decided to leave, believing that Wright would soon get killed, as everybody, almost, was mad with him. We started to where Morgan T. Reynolds was teaching school. It was a cold morning; we went across the hill and down by Bill Johnson's, then up the main Boone creek to just in front of Quiller Bentley's dwelling house. Here we met W. S. Wright. There being a short curve in the road we couldn't see each other until he was within fifteen steps of us. He probably saw us first. When I first saw him he was riding towards us pretty fast and drawing his 45 Colts. I could see determination in his eye. In a thought I raised my Winchester, brother John doing the same, both firing at the same time. Wright reeled and fell from his horse. We stayed a few minutes until Quiller Bentley could get there to take charge of his body. We then went to the top of the hill above where brother Bill lived. John went down and got Bill and we all went to Squire Quillens and gave up. He placed us in the custody of the constable, Albert Evans. Each side mustered about thirty men. We went to Whitesburg to have our trial before County Judge Blair. We went into trial, but before it ended circuit court convened, it having jurisdiction over the county court, the case was transferred on motion of the commonwealth. The grand jury investigating the case, after examining about one hundred witnesses, reported on the twelfth day of the term, releasing us on the grounds of self defense. The commonwealth filed an affidavit against the report of the grand jury, asking the court to hold us under bond until the next term of court. The court sustained the motion and held us in a bond of $1000.

We returned home, knowing that the trouble was not at an end, but had just begun. Everything went along quietly for some time. I moved to Rockhouse creek, about eight miles away from the Wright settlement. When the timber put out the trouble began anew. Tilden and William Wright, whose blood was hot over the killing of their father and hopeless condition of the prosecution, determined to avenge the death of their father. Armed with the guns of which they had about $500 worth, they began ambushing, firing at long range at us everytime they got in sight of us.

JOHN'S AND MY INDICTMENT AND CHANGE OF VENIRE.

The court convened; the grand jury found an indictment for murder against me and John. The judge sent me word that we were indicted and for us to come on to court, which we did, and answered to our indictments, insisting on trial at this term of court. The commonwealth filed an affidavit asking for a change of venire. Their plea was that the commonwealth could not get a fair and impartial trial in Letcher county on account of the great malice which existed in this county against W. S. Wright.

The court sustained the motion of the commonwealth. The commonwealth and defense failed to agree as to what county the case should be sent for trial. Then the court decided to transfer the case to Pineville, the county seat of Bell county, Ky., requiring a bond of $1000 each for our appearance at Pineville at the next term of their county court. The bond was immediately made, as quite a number of our most wealthy and influential men rose up and asked for their names to be put on the bond. This seemed to arouse the ambition of my friends, seeing how the opposition had taken advantage of me in having the case transferred to another county where Wright's bad reputation was not known.

In the spring of 1901, Wm. Wright waylaid our cousin, Nat Bentley, where he was splitting rails and shot a hole through his hat. By this time affairs had gotten so critical our friends were forced to have guards around their fields—some doing guard while others worked.

Nat Bently came and got me and John to guard his field while he worked. He was getting behind with his crop. Soon one morning we saw Wm. Wright slipping up a spur to where mother and Tilden McFalls lived. I was watching him through a field glass. He was about eight hundred yards from us. I saw him step to the side of a tree and begin shooting in the direction of mother's house at Tilden McFall. He fired six shots scaring his (McFall's) wife, causing an untimely birth. I raised the sights of my gun to try him a pop, but John said "Don't shoot, you will waste your cartridge; he is too far away." He was indicted for this, but beat the case by getting killed before his trial. The next day he went up the same ridge with his gun. He set my fence afire and I fired two shots at him, running him away, and the fire burned two hundred panels of his own fence, each party being afraid to go and put the fire out. I saw him run into a bunch of thick bushes, and I hallooed to him and told him to go home and lay down his gun. I told him if he did not he was going to get killed.

He said, "I knew you would, for you killed my father, and I know you would kill me if you could get a chance." I said, "I can if I have to, but I would rather not." These were the last words we ever spoke.

Bell county court was drawing near. I started to Whitesburg to get summonses for some witnesses. On my way I fell in company with Judge J. A. Craft, who was riding along the road just above the mouth of Colly Creek. Looking down the road about a hundred yards in front of us, we saw James Johnson, Tilden and Wm. Wright coming toward us. Craft said, "Yonder comes three of your enemies; you will have trouble with them." Said I, "Maybe not." I looked at Craft; he was pale. Said I, "If you are afraid you can drop behind and I will do the best I can." I got my gun, expecting to have to fight for my life. Craft rode by my side, between them and me, stopping just as we passed them. I rode on, looking back and keeping my eyes on them until I got some distance from them. Craft came on. Overtaking me, he said, "Noah, I want you to go back another way; don't go back up the river. I don't like the way those fellows talked to me." They asked him where I was going. He said to Whitesburg, I think. They asked, "When is he coming back?" He said, "I don't know."

I went on to town, attended to my business, and on my return home, thinking of what Craft had said, when I came to the mouth of Colly's Creek I decided to go up the river. Coming in sight of Mary Jane Bates' house, I saw three men leaving whom I took to be my enemies. I then believed I would have to come in contact with them.

I thought of going up Cram Creek to avoid them. However, I decided to go the near way and take chances with them. I was now at the foot of a little hill riding pretty fast. Up and along the top of the hill I came to where the brush and ivy was pretty thick, expecting them to attack me any minute. I carried my revolver in my hand. All at once a voice rang out, "Halt!" Looking in that direction I saw Tilden Wright pointing his pistol at me. We fired at the same time. The shooting became general—they all shooting at me and me at them. Wm. Wright, jumping into the road, caught at my horse's bridle. I fired at his head, shooting him through the nose. When he fell to the ground the shooting then ceased. My horse, which had been excited, jumped back and forth and began running at full speed. A short distance on my way I saw some ivy bushes shake, I fired at them and a mule reared and fell. Checking my horse at the foot of the hill to examine him and see if he was shot, I found that only two bullets had hit and scarred my saddle. Going on to Abraham Potter's, where my brother John and other friends were, upon entering the room they said they smelled powder. They asked, "Have you spilt powder on yourself?" I said "No, but the Wrights have spilt a lot of it on me." We began to search for bullet holes and found several in my overcoat. Then I showed them my shirt, where a bullet had cut my shirt bosom. Morton Potter asked, "What has become of your mustache?" I said, "I lost it on the ridge, below Wiley Webb's. I have had a pretty close call, but I am still living."

John said, "We will make it d— hot for them between now and this time tomorrow." So we planned a raid on the W. S. Wright fort.

John, our friends and myself started pretty soon for the "fort." Reaching the "fort" before daylight, we located ourselves on a ridge nearby, watching until about 9:00 o'clock the next day. We saw no one except some small boys. Believing they were in the house, John said, "Do you see those three cows standing there. Let us all fire at them; that will start it." We all fired and the three cows fell dead. In an instant the bullets came whistling by our heads. We returned the fire, sending bullets through the doors, windows, and anywhere we thought a weak place. The shooting lasted about an hour. Then we went to our mother's house and got our dinner.

Returning in the evening, we gave them a few rounds. Then leaving our breastworks we went down a lane near Ezekiel Bentley's. Seeing one of the Wrights coming out from his home, I raised my gun, caught a bead and fired at him a distance of three hundred yards. He jumped from his horse, ran through a mill dam to the house. The men in the house hearing the shot, began to fire at us. We returned the fire and the shooting then stopped, and we went on up Boone, learning later that two of them were wounded.

"DEVIL" JOHN WRIGHT ORGANIZES A BAND OF TWENTY-ONE MEN.

On hearing of this, about the same number of men joined me, one of which, Creed Potter, was as brave a man as ever lived in the mountains of Kentucky. I called a meeting and we had a conference. My men disagreed as to the right way to conduct our warfare, as all knew that going against John Wright was no pink tea party. John Reynolds and Creed Potter decided to go in a gang by themselves. The reader knows, or should know, that there are always spies and traitors in all feudish warfare like this. Now, John Wright, learning of our disagreement, took advantage of the situation and placed his men in a gap in the mountain between Millstone and Boone Creek, expecting Reynolds and Potter to come along at any minute. John Wright, using his field-glasses, saw them coming up the mountain about three-quarters of a mile away. Reynolds and Potter had been informed that "Devil" John Wright and about twenty-one men were in this mountain looking for them.

Reynolds and Potter, seeing plenty of fresh signs, turned to the left and were coming around a high point in the mountain. When Wright saw they were coming through that gap, he took his men over the knob and met them on the side of the knob. Reynolds and Potter, looking up, saw Wright and his men coming. John Reynolds said, "Yonder they come." About this time Wrights fired a volley at them. Reynolds raised his gun, fired and mortally wounding Wm. Wright, then ran up the spur, taking shelter behind an oak tree, Creed Potter taking shelter behind a chestnut tree. Reynolds would spring in behind his tree, wrench his gun, then spring out and fire. He fired five shots, killing and wounding five men. At this time he received a shot which broke his right arm just above the elbow, disabling him so that he could not use his gun. He left the tree and ran down the hill, leaving his partner to fight by himself. Potter fought until his ammunition gave out and then went in pursuit of Reynolds, tracking him by the blood and expecting to find him dead. But Reynolds had reached the main road and had taken up his stand at Jeff Bentley's for a second fight, where Potter rejoined him.

Wm. Wright died at 4:00 o'clock the next morning.

McCoy and Beverly were picked up dead on the ground.

Isaac Mills and Elkins were wounded but recovered.

I was on my way to meet John Reynolds at the head of the river where we had an agreement to meet. I heard shooting, knew it was a fight and turned back in that direction and met a friend coming after me who said, "Your brother John Reynolds is wounded and wants you." I dashed away at full speed and in fifteen minutes was with him.

My men, hearing the fight, rallied together, about twenty of them, and joined us. Reynolds was badly wounded. We carried him up to where I lived on the farm of my Uncle Joe Reynolds. I sent for Dr. Joe McQuary. John Wright now procured warrants for John Reynolds, Creed Potter, myself, and seven or eight others of my men. He also went to the Governor and got rewards signed for all of us.

On the hearing of Wright procuring rewards from the Governor, I got the sheriff to come to my house, where John was in bed wounded, and we surrendered ourselves to him. So the doctor, sheriff, and judge all came together.

The doctor said it would be dangerous to force him (my brother) to go to town on account of his present condition. The sheriff didn't know what to do. I suggested to leave a deputy to guard him, but no man would stay. So I said to sheriff, "If you will trust me I will take care of him and when the doctor says it will be safe I will bring him to town." On this we agreed. I was sworn in and given a written statement showing my authority. "Devil" John Wright, on hearing this, got very angry and told the sheriff that I didn't intend to bring John Reynolds in, and had taken advantage of him. He tried to get the sheriff to countermand the order. The sheriff could not. The next move John

Wright made was by false reports to get the Governor to issue an order to send the State militia. Upon learning of this fact I sent one of my men, B. M. Webb, to consult with the Governor, relating the facts in the case. The Governor countermanded the order. So John Wright was defeated in that scheme.

THE NEXT MOVE HE MADE

There was what we called a pistol deputy sheriff, one John Elkins, who mustered fifteen men, and said he would come and take my wounded brother, John, to town. I heard he was coming and was watching for him. I saw him and his men coming and told my brother to be quiet, that I would attend to them. I picked up my Winchester rifle, walked into the front yard and stepped to the side of an apple tree. As they rode up I raised my gun to my shoulder and said, "Have you men lived as long as you want to? If you have, the one that wants to die first start to get down."

"We don't want any trouble," was the answer." I said, "If you don't, ride on down the road." So they went on down the road, thinking I had several men in the background. The next news was: Alex Wright, who was friendly with both sides, came and said, "Noah, I don't take any sides in this trouble. John Wright has sent me to tell you if you would give up he would see that you was treated with kindness, and if you would not he had thirty men ready at Bob Johnson's (about one-half a mile distant), and for your women and children to get out of the way."

He was coming to take us by force. I said, "Tell 'Old' John that I had done nothing to give up for, and that he didn't want to do anything but kill me," that "I will not agree to that. Tell him to come on and be in front and don't do as he has always done, push other men in front and get them killed, and then prosecute somebody for defending themselves. Our women and children will be taken care of." There was a small brick house near the dwelling house. I took brick out of the wall, making holes about eight inches square, to shoot through. I placed my guns and men in readiness for the attack. I hung lanterns to give light at night, so they couldn't slip up and dynamite our house, as it was reported that that was their intention.

We held this position for about twenty days. "Old" John failed to come.

The doctor said John must have an operation. We not being able to get another doctor to come to our place, as most everybody was afraid to come, I then took John to Whitesburg, as I had agreed to do and had an operation performed, and he got well. The court found indictments against John and Creed Potter for the killing of Wm. Wright. These indictments were transferred to Pineville, Bell county, where our other cases awaited trial. John and Creed surrendered to these indictments and went on to Bell county for trial. They were tried, convicted and sentenced to the penitentiary for fifteen years each. John Reynolds was soon pardoned by Governor Beckham. Creed Potter made his escape from prison and was never recaptured.

FIRST TRIP TO BELL COUNTY COURT

We all left our homes in Kentucky to go to court in Bell county, all armed with revolvers. Both factions met at Norton, Va., where we were to take the train—about one hundred men and women, all mad. Once in a while some of the women would say something that looked like it would start trouble. We all procured tickets. Train time came. We started to board the train. Joe Doody being the conductor (and a mighty fine man) and fearing there was going to be trouble, said "I am afraid I can't take you all on this train at this time. Mr. Reynolds, won't you wait until tomorrow?" I said "I would rather not, as I am under bond to appear in court in the morning, and I don't want to give my bondsman any trouble. I will promise you on my part that I, nor none of my men, won't have any trouble if some one else don't start it." Then John Wright stepped up and said, Mr. Doody, I don't think there will be any trouble. When we fight we fight, and when we law we law." I then said, "John Wright, you take your men in one coach and I will take mine in the other." Then Mr. Doody agreed to let us board the train knowing John Wright and I had bought all our tickets in clubs together. Not many passengers boarded the train that night, as the news went on ahead that the Reynolds and Wright feudists were on the train. We reached Pineville without trouble.

THE NEXT TROUBLE OF ANY CONSEQUENCE

We all returned to our respective homes in Kentucky. Brother John and Creed Potter, my best, truest and tried friends, being sent to the penitentiary, I lost my best counsel.

At this time I was living on Potter's Fork of Boone Creek, now known as Haymen, and two miles above my own home. I decided to move back home where I was raised. Loading up two wagons with a part of my household goods, I hired Marion Hall and John Potter to drive the teams. Starting down Boone Creek I asked Potter if he had his nerve. He said he had and always carried it with him. I said, "As likely as not you will need it, for I am expecting trouble." We went on in the direction of Lettie Wright's, having to go by where she lived to get to my place. She had learned that I was moving back and had placed her men in ambush near the road. I was walking through the field a near way. My wagons and drivers being between me and the men who were in ambush. All at once a keen crack from a rifle rang out. I saw my drivers jump from their wagons. Marion Hall began shooting at them. The teams ran away. Me and my friend, T. P. McFalls, armed with Winchesters, began firing at them in ambush. Hall shot his gun empty, and was slightly wounded. He ran away back up the road. Me and McFalls took shelter in a ditch, being some hundred yards away. I now began firing my gun, which shot explosive balls, at rocks close behind them, making it so hot for them they had to leave their hiding places, and as they would go over the hill McFall would try them a pop. This lasted about one-half an hour. We crawled out at the end of the ditch which led out into some bushes in the direction of Lettie Wright's house. As we were going up a little rise a shot was fired which passed through my hat and slightly wounding McFalls. From this point I saw some men carrying a wounded man from where they had run across the ridge, in the direction of John Bates' house. I could also see my teams. They had stopped in the lower end of the bottom. Leaving them in the hands of my enemies, I started back up the creek, looking after my drivers, expecting to find them shot. After going some distance we came in sight of where they were in ambush, a little higher up on the ridge. Several shots were fired at us from long range, but with no effect.

Potter, one of my drivers, had lost his hat. I asked him where his hat was and he said he had left it to take care of his team. We went on up the creek to the mouth of Potter's Creek. My men, about ten in number, one of which was an officer, had collected together. We all started back down the creek and found our wagons and teams unharmed. My drivers got their teams and we all went on by Lettie Wright's to my home. I never heard who the wounded man was or how badly he was wounded.

MY TRIAL AT PINEVILLE, KENTUCKY, FOR THE MURDER OF W. S. WRIGHT

At the regular term of court my trial came up, the jury was impanelled, the commonwealth and defense answered ready. The trial lasted fourteen days. The jury returned a verdict of guilty, giving me a life sentence. I took the case before the court of appeals. This court affirmed the judgment of the lower court, and on April 2, 1902, I was taken to the penitentiary. I served as a trusty prisoner in a suit of honor. I petitioned Governor Beckham for a pardon. He refused to grant it. He had already granted a pardon to Brother John some time before I put my application in. I was held in prison until Govenor Augustus E. Wilson succeeded Governor Beckham. On January 1st, 1909, he pardoned me from the charge of killing W. S. Wright. I rejoined my family, who had now moved to Knott county, Kentucky, bought them a farm on a creek known as Little Betty Troublesome, where I now live with and amongst a host of friends.

John H. Reynolds, returning home from prison, went to the State of Virginia to live. Marrying Miss Carrie Addington, the daughter of Philmore Addington, he lived a quiet and peaceable life. He served as police at Jenkins, Kentucky, about three years, then was appointed as prohibition agent for the eastern part of Kentucky, served about two years, his headquarters being at Lexington, Kentucky. His home now was at Pikesville, Kentucky. On a raid in Johnson county, Kentucky, after a band of moonshiners, came in contact with a band of the McKenseys, who were moonshiners and headed by Joseph Paton McKensey. He was killed on the 26th day of August, 1921. Six of these moonshiners are serving life terms in the penitentiary for his murder.

Mountain Feuds of Kentucky

I was converted in the year 1914, and joined the regular Baptist church. The church very soon authorized me to preach. My church is one of the largest in the mountains, having one hundred and forty-seven members, and belongs to the Indian Bottom Association. My lot has been cast as a minister of the Gospel in the mountain parts of Kentucky. Tilden Wright, my old enemy, W. S. Wright's oldest son, joined the church the same day that I did. He joined the Thornton church of Indian Bottom Association. Our churches are of the same faith and order, and our associations have fellowship with each other. His church authorized him to preach. We often meet and preach together.

SERMON

Dear reader, I wish to leave now here with you a sermon on the great mission Christ gave to his Apostles.

What I shall use for a text, or a ground on which I will base my remarks, will be found in the 28th and last chapter of Matthew, beginning at the 18th verse, including the remainder of the chapter: "And Jesus came and spake unto them, saying, All power is given unto me in heaven and in earth. Go ye therefore, and teach all nations, baptizing them in the name of the Father, and of the Son, and of the Holy Ghost, teaching them to observe all things whatsoever I have commanded you, and lo, I am with you alway, even until the end of the world. Amen."

Now, the first thing we must consider is that Jesus is here giving his disciples, or called ministers, a charge or mission reaching the end of the world, and it goes to all nations. And he lets them know that He has the right to send them, and that no one else has, by telling them that all power was given Him in heaven and in earth. God the Father had given it to His son, Jesus Christ, the mediator between God and man. He here uses the words power, heaven and earth, giving them to understand that when He went to heaven that He would also be with them on earth. This may look strange to some one, but it's not to me. We see that Jesus told His Disciples that He and His Father were one—I in the Father, the Father in me; I in you and you in me. This being true, He could tell them, lo, I am with you to the end of the world. Thus, He gave them to understand that through His power they would be able to fill the mission. The next thing we will look into, He told them to teach all nations, baptizing them in the name of the Father and of the Son and of the Holy Ghost. We must consider it would be impossible for them to have done this except they had the baptism to baptize with. Jesus had promised them that He would send them another comforter, which was the Holy Ghost—said when He is come He will guide you in the way of all truth, and bring to memory all things whatsoever I have said unto you. This Holy Ghost is what Jesus commanded them to Baptize with, or in the name of. So before we can preach the Gospel of the Kingdom we must be in possession of the power that God gave to His Son, Jesus, both in heaven and in earth. We find in Luke the 24th chapter, 45th verse: "Then opened He their understanding, that they might understand the Scriptures, and said unto them, thus it is written, and thus it behooved Christ to suffer, and to rise from the dead the third day; and that repentance and remissions of sins should be preached in His name among all nations, beginning at Jerusalem. And, behold, I send the promise of my Father upon you: but tarry ye in the city of Jerusalem, until ye be endued with power from on high." Here is the power that God gave the Son to give to his called ministers, that would enable them to preach or teach all nations and enable them to fill their mission to Baptize in the name of the Father and Son and Holy Ghost. We further find in the

22nd chapter of the Acts of the Apostles, after Christ ascended to the Father, that on the day of Pentecost and suddenly there came a sound from heaven as of a mighty rushing wind and it filled all the house where they were sitting, and there appeared unto them cloven tongues like as of fire and it set upon each of them and they were all filled with the Holy Ghost. This was the promise of the Father that He had given to His Son to give to His ministers or teachers that would enable them to fill their calling and to Baptize in the name of the Father, Son and Holy Ghost, and then could teach them all things whatsoever He had said unto them—the power that the Jesus said was given Him in heaven and in earth, was the Gospel of the Apostle Paul, declaring it to be the power of God unto salvation to everyone that believed, first to the Jew and then to the Greek, for, therein is the righteousness of God revealed from faith to faith.

We then see the great necessity of preaching the Gospel. The Apostle Paul said faith comes by hearing and hearing by the word of God. And how can you hear without a preacher, and how can you preach except you be sent. This gives us to understand that no man can preach except God sends him and Jesus, who has all power in heaven and earth, gives him the power and He is the power; that is why He said, "And lo, I am with you even to the end of the world." We find when His disciples asked Him to teach them how to pray, in the conclusion said, "Thine is the power and glory forever, Amen!" We then find in the writings of St. Mark, in the 16th chapter, beginning at the 15th verse, "And He said unto them, go ye into all the world and preach the Gospel to every creature. He that believeth and is baptized shall be saved; but he that believeth not, shall be damned." This shows us the justification in the condemnation of the people that will not believe. The Gospel is being preached through all the world, including every creature. No one is left with any excuse to plead in the day of judgment. How shall the people know the Gospel? By the power. We find in this same chapter: "Signs shall follow them; In my name shall they cast out devils."

The Gospel casts out devils, it being the power of God, and this gives the sinner power to repent and believe and this leaves the responsibility on the people. Jesus said the Gospel of this Kingdom shall be preached in all the world for a witness, and then the end shall come. So, dear friends, these words which I have written will live in the memory of some one after I am dead and my soul or spirit is lingering under the altar of God, saying: Oh, most holy God almighty, how long will it be until thou wilt avenge our blood on them that dwell on the earth? Amen.

www.ingramcontent.com/pod-product-compliance
Lightning Source LLC
Chambersburg PA
CBHW030141100526
44592CB00011B/988